Absolute Crime Presents:

Cells in Hell

The 15 Worst Prisons On Earth

ABSO UTE
CR ME

By William Webb

Absolute Crime Books

www.absolutecrime.com

Table of Contents

About Us

Absolute Crime publishes only the best true crime literature. Our focus is on the crimes that you've probably never heard of, but you are fascinated to read more about. With each engaging and gripping story, we try to let readers relive moments in history that some people have tried to forget.

Remember, our books are not meant for the faint at heart. We don't hold back—if a crime is bloody, we let the words splatter across the page so you can experience the crime in the most horrifying way!

If you enjoy this book, please visit our homepage to see other books we offer; if you have any feedback, we'd love to hear from you!

Introduction

Some prisons are so famous that they become household names. Alcatraz, Sing Sing, Supermax, Pelican Bay, Angola, Bang Kwang, and Petak Island are known all over the world. These prisons are well known because they have a reputation for being tough and, in some cases, escape-proof.

Many prisons are also well known for brutality and violence. Venezuela's Maracaibo Prison has a reputation for being the world's most violent prison. Carandiru Penitentiary in Brazil became so infamous that the government tore it down in order to avoid controversy.

A few prisons are so tough that even hardened criminals are afraid to be sentenced to them. Such facilities include the Louisiana State Penitentiary at Angola, Pelican, the federal Supermax maintained by the U.S. Justice Department, and Russia's Petak Island.

There are also some prisons that are simply huge. Angola and Riker's Island in New York City are large enough to be considered communities in their own right. The sheer size of those operations makes them notable.

Some prisons are known for controversy, including Guantanamo Bay, Pelican Bay, and Gldani Prison in the nation of Georgia. Guantanamo Bay and Gldani have become the centers of political controversies that have not been resolved.

Worst of all are those prisons that exist solely for the purpose of oppression and depriving innocent people of their freedom. Such facilities include North Korea's Camp 22, Drapchi Prison in Tibet, and the notorious Tadmoor Prison in Syria. Those prisons house mostly innocent people whose only crime was to oppose a dictatorship.

Yet all of these prisons have one thing in common: They instill fear. At the end of the day the purpose of any prison is the creation of fear. It is that fear that makes prisons so fascinating even to law-abiding citizens. Yes, prisons are typically places of fear, but the prisons listed in this book are among the scariest on Earth.

ADX Supermax

America's most famous modern prison might be the most secure prison ever built. Even its name strikes fear into the hearts of some of the world's toughest terrorists and gangsters: Supermax. Supermax has become just as famous as its predecessor, Alcatraz, and just as infamous.

Supermax was built to house prisoners that are too dangerous or violent to be housed in traditional maximum security facilities. The official name of the facility is the Administration Maximum Facility, or ADX. Supermax is actually a nickname for the facility used by the press. It is an abbreviation of the phrase "super maximum security."

It is located in rural Freemont County, Colo., just outside the town of Florence. Despite what some people think, Supermax is not located in the mountains; instead, it's in the Arkansas River Valley that is south of Colorado Springs and east of Pueblo. Many people think Supermax is in the mountains because it has the nickname "the Alcatraz of the Rockies," but in reality, Supermax is about 40 miles from the Rocky Mountains.

Housing the Worst of the Worst

The U.S. Federal Bureau of Prisons built Supermax in 1994 when it realized it was losing control of cellblocks to a violent new generation of criminals. Events that triggered its construction included riots, the murders of two prison guards, and an incident in which three of the men who bombed the World Trade Center in 1993 wrote to other terrorists abroad.

The Bureau realized that they needed a new kind of prison for these criminals. The idea was to create a prison in which inmates would be under permanent lockdown. All the prisoners in one section of the facility, called the "control unit," would be kept in solitary confinement. They would have no contact with other prisoners to protect themselves and others.

Part of the reason for this is to keep those prisoners from being killed in the general population. Another is to prevent gang wars and other violent outbursts. Authorities are afraid that terrorists, gang bosses, spies, and other celebrity criminals will be targeted for death by gang members and other troublemakers if they are in the general population.

Life in Supermax

The big difference between Supermax and a traditional prison is that most of the inmates spend all their time in solitary confinement. Most of the prisoners are there because of the problems they would create in traditional prisons. That includes those with a high risk of escape and prisoners that are violent and uncontrollable.

Life in Supermax is extraordinarily harsh. Prisoners spend almost all their time in 7-foot by 12-foot cells. Each cell contains nothing but a bed, a toilet, and a shower. Food is inserted through a slot in the solid metal door, which means the prisoners never go to a cafeteria to eat. The idea is to keep the prisoners from communicating with each other and organizing themselves into gangs.

The prisoners can only leave their cells for specific purposes, such as to see a lawyer, get medical care, or exercise. They can exercise in a small yard, but that's the only time they get to see the sun. Most of the prisoners spend all their time in those cells.

Celebrity Inmates

Like Alcatraz, Supermax is famous because many of its inmates are famous, or rather infamous, criminals. Some of the crooks who have taken up residence there are household names.

Famous Supermax inmates and former inmates include:

Unabomber Theodore Kazynski, Oklahoma City bomber Terry L. Nichols, traitorous former FBI agent Robert Hanssen, Zacharias Mossaoui (widely believed to be part of the plot behind the Sept. 11 attacks), Timothy McVeigh (who was executed for the Oklahoma City bombing), Ramzi Yousef (the mastermind behind the 1993 World Trade Center bombing), Larry Hoover (the boss of the notorious Gangster Disciples gang), and Barry Mills and Tyler Bingham (who are believed to be leaders of the feared Aryan Nation, a racist prison gang). Shoe bomber Richard Reid and Atlanta Olympic bomber Eric Rudolf are also housed there.

A number of prisoners are there because they are also well-known escape artists that have broken out of other prisons. Some of the other criminals housed there are particularly fearsome. Racist cult leader Dwight York is serving a sentence for racketeering, for using his followers as slaves, and for child molestation. Another racist cult leader, Matthew Hale, is serving a 40-year term for hiring a hitman to kill a federal judge. Former federal corrections officer (prison guard) Michael Rudkin is serving a 90-year sentence for having sex with an inmate and trying to hire a hitman to kill a federal agent and his ex-wife.

Other inmates include the leaders of some of the nation's worst prison gangs, including the Mexican Mafia, the Aryan Brotherhood, the Latin Kings, and the Nuestra Family. Several drug cartel leaders and former Bonanno crime family boss Vincent Basciano are also locked up there.

A Prison That's Too Tough

Many civil liberties advocates believe that Supermax is too harsh. Their argument is that Supermax violates the United States Constitution, specifically with regard to cruel and unusual punishment. The critics have labeled the solitary confinement program at Supermax as cruel and unusual. These criticisms haven't convinced U.S. courts to shut the prison down.

Even though it isn't popular, Supermax will probably stay in operation for the foreseeable future. It exists because the U.S. prison population is so vast that a special prison is needed for criminals that even the prison system cannot control.

Bibliography

Pilkington, E. (2012, April 10). ADX Florence Supermax Prison: the Alcatraz of the Rockies. Retrieved July 22, 2013, from The Guardian: http://www.guardian.co.uk/world/2012/apr/10/abu-hamza-isolation-supermax-prison

Vick, K. (2007, September 30). Isolating the Menace in a Sterile Supermax. Retrieved July 22, 2013, from The Washington Post: http://www.washingtonpost.com/wp-dyn/content/article/2007/09/29/AR2007092900928.html?sid=ST2007093000318

Wikipedia (n.d.). ADX Florence. Retrieved July 22, 2013, from Wikipedia: http://en.wikipedia.org/wiki/ADX_Florence

Angola

The Louisiana State Penitentiary popularly known as Angola is famous for two things: a reputation for inhumane treatment of prisoners and a rodeo. The prison is so large that the US Postal Service considers it a community and gave it a post office named Angola. Angola was also the name of a plantation that existed on the same location before the prison opened.

Angola has long had a reputation as America's toughest state prison and has been nicknamed the Alcatraz of the South because it is bordered on three sides by the Mississippi River. Many prison employees can only reach their jobs by a special ferry service. Angola is the largest prison in the United States, housing 5,000 inmates on 18,000 acres. It isn't the largest penal facility in the U.S. however; Riker's Island in New York City houses more prisoners, but it is a jail and not a prison.

Angola Prison is so large that it actually has its own airstrip. The strip is used by private planes that haul prisoners to and from the facility. State officials sometimes fly in and out of the airstrip as well.

Angola opened for business in 1901, although prisoners were housed there when Major Samuel James ran a plantation on the property in the late 19th century. James leased convicts from the State to work his land. The state bought Angola, which is named for the country in Africa, from the James family in 1901.

Hell at Angola

Angola has long been known as one of America's toughest prisons. During the 1930s hardened criminals would break down in tears if they heard they'd be sent there. The authors of a biography of Leadbelly, a famous musician who was incarcerated at Angola in the 1930s, described it as being as close to slavery as anybody could come in America in 1930.

In the 1940s a former prisoner named William Sadler wrote a series of articles called *Hell at Angola* in an attempt to get reform. By 1952 conditions were so bad that 31 inmates cut their Achilles tendons so they wouldn't have to work at Angola. The prisoners did this because all inmates at Angola were expected to work like slaves in the fields.

Another horror at Angola was sexual slavery; during the 1960s and 1970s inmates kept other inmates as sex slaves. The slaves were gang raped and traded like cattle among the inmates. C. Murray Henderson, who served as Warden at the time, believed the guards sanctioned the sex slave system.

The prison was particularly brutal because most of the guards were prisoners themselves. Inmates would be given special favors if they would force their fellow prisoners to work. Prisoners had to work in the sugar mill, a ranch, a dairy, a cannery, and the farms. The prisoners had to grow their own food and were required to work 12 hours a day in the 1930s.

Conditions Don't Change

Angola's reputation for inhumane treatment is just as strong as ever. In July 2013 newspapers reported that Congressman Cedric Richmond had sent a letter to the U.S. Justice Department asking for an investigation of Angola. Richmond was especially critical of the solitary confinement system.

The solitary confinement area at Angola is called "the Dungeon" by prisoners and guards. Many prisoners in Angola are kept on extended lockdown. There are reportedly around 100 extended lockdown cells at Angola.

Conditions for prisoners have improved somewhat; most Angola inmates now live in air conditioned dormitories. Prisoners can theoretically use the recreational facilities at Butler Park on the prison grounds, which has barbecue kits and picnic tables.

Resort for the Staff

One reason why Angola has attracted so much criticism is the special amenities available to the prison staff. Guards and administrators at Angola enjoy a lot of luxuries normally available only to guests at luxury resorts.

These amenities include Lake Killarney, a private lake stocked with crappie fish, a nine-hole golf course, a swimming pool, and a tennis court. Prisoners are not allowed to play on the golf course or fish in the lake. The public can play on the course, but you need to pass a background check to reach it.

There's also the Ranch House, a private clubhouse where guards and wardens hang out. The Ranch House is a conference center that includes guest quarters with a bedroom and fireplace. There's also a dining room where inmate cooks prepare special meals for the warden and guests. The food was so good that many of the cooks at the Ranch House later worked as cooks at the Governor's Mansion in Baton Rouge.

Angola Inc.

Angola is not just a prison; it's actually a giant factory farm and a complex of manufacturing businesses. It has 2,000 heads of cattle and a farm that produces four million pounds of vegetables a year. Peppers, okra, onions, soybeans, squash, tomatoes, and cabbage are all grown there as well as cotton, corn, and wheat. All of the farm work at Angola is done by inmates, who also participate in the prison's famous rodeo.

Agriculture isn't the only business at Angola; there's a mattress factory, a mop and broom factory, a sign factory, and a license plate factory so big that it makes plates for some customers in foreign countries. Coffins for prisoners are also manufactured at the prison.

Angola is also the only prison in the United States to have its own radio station, which broadcasts mostly Christian programming. There's also a magazine called *The Angolite*, which has won awards for its writing.

Angola the Attraction

The most famous event at Angola is the Rodeo, which is held on every Sunday in April through October. The Rodeo attracts thousands of visitors to a 10,000-seat arena specially built for it. During the Rodeo prisoners sell food to visitors at concession stands. The money is handled by the guards. The Rodeo also features an Arts and Crafts festival.

Angola is one of the few working prisons that is also a tourist attraction. An Angola museum housed just outside the prison's boundaries features such exhibits as Gruesome Gertie, the State of Louisiana's infamous electric chair.

Angola isn't just America's largest prison; it may be its most unusual. No other penal facility in the United States contains a farm, a rodeo, and a radio station, although several have its reputation for brutality.

Bibliography

McGaughy, L. (2013, July 12). Angola prison conditions 'inhumane,' should be subject to justice investigation Richmond says. Retrieved July 25, 2013, from The Times Picayune: http://www.nola.com/crime/index.ssf/2013/07/angola_prison_conditions_inhum.html

Wikipedia(n.d.). Louisiana State Penitentiary. Retrieved July 25, 2013, from Wikipedia: http://en.wikipedia.org/wiki/Louisiana_State_Penitentiary

Bang Kwang Central Prison in Thailand

Unlike most penal facilities in Southeast Asia, Bang Kwang Central Prison in Thailand, just outside Bangkok, is well known to foreigners. The prison was the basis of an Australian TV show that helped launch Nicole Kidman's career, and it has even been featured in the *Mafia Wars* computer games.

Bang Kwang is one of the few Asian prisons that have a reputation outside of its country. It is also one of the only prisons in Asia that houses more than a few European and American inmates.

Bang Kwang is well known outside Thailand because American, Australian, and British citizens have been imprisoned there on drug charges. Thailand is a well-known center of the illegal drug trade, even though its laws harshly punish drug offenders. Australians even have a nickname for Bang Kwang, calling it "the Bangkok Hilton."

The Big Tiger

The Thai nickname for Bang Kwang is even more colorful and frightening—"the Big Tiger." The Big Tiger has a reputation for being Thailand's toughest and most secure prison. It houses the country's death row and regularly plays home to some of the most dangerous prisoners, including drug-dealing gangsters, from all over the world.

Bang Kwang is an extremely harsh environment and hardly a fun place to visit. The only food prisoners receive is one bowl of rice and one bowl of vegetable soup a day. Inmates that want more to eat have to buy food from the prison's canteen. Foreign prisoners are provided extra food and money by charities. The British Embassy provides food and vitamins to British subjects doing time there.

Prisoners do get some amenities not available in American prisons, including their own cooking facilities. They even get butane gas to work with in some of the cells. Not surprisingly, wealthy prisoners, such as gang bosses, often live well in Bang Kwang.

Part of the reason Bang Kwang is so harsh is that poorer prisoners end up as virtual slaves of wealthier inmates. They end up having to do chores and worse to get extra food.

The Bangkok Hilton

Bang Kwang got increasingly crowded after 2003 when the Thai government passed harsh new drug laws. The new prisoners included Michael Connell, a supermarket employee from Manchester, England, who was tricked into being a courier for drug runners.

Connell was interviewed there by the BBC, which became the first news organization to visit "the Bangkok Hilton" in 2004. Connell told reporters that he slept in a dormitory with 1,000 other men and he earned extra food by teaching his fellow prisoners English.

The BBC also reported that order in "the Hilton" is maintained by the Blue Shirts, a group of tough inmates that are given special privileges if they assist the guards. This is a variation of the Block Warden system used in American prisons until the 1980s. Under that system, a tough prisoner, usually a gang member, was put in charge of a cellblock. If the prisoner kept order, he got special privileges, such as a TV set in his cell, from the guards.

The Ghost Gate and Other Bizarre Happenings at the Bang Kwang Central Prison

The BBC also revealed how Thailand's death row worked. The condemned would be notified of execution just two hours before receiving a lethal injection. Prisoners would receive their last rites from a Buddhist monk, who helped their souls pass through the ghost gate to the next life.

A 2012 *Bangkok Post* article described the last executioner at Bang Kwang, Chaovaret Jaruboon, as a gentle man who played in a rock band in his spare time. Part of Jaruboon's job was to fire 10–15 bullets into the back of a condemned prisoner who was strapped to what the *Post* described as a cross. This method was later replaced by lethal injection.

The BBC also found some bizarre things happening at Bang Kwang, including a television station and special quarters for transvestites. The prisoners apparently had their own TV station, complete with makeup artists.

More disturbing was the prison hospital where inmates were kept chained to beds. A prison doctor told reporters that he was short on medicine because most Thais don't like donating anything to prisoners. Instead, they think those imprisoned in Bang Kwang deserve to be there and deserve to suffer.

There is one thing that prisoners at Bang Kwang want more than anything else: a letter from His Majesty the King of Thailand. The King has the ability to pardon prisoners, and he occasionally does.

On Television

A 1980s Australian TV miniseries called *Bangkok Hilton* featured a harsh Thai prison modeled on Bang Kwang in which an innocent Australian woman was imprisoned. The series was notable for featuring a very young Nicole Kidman in a supporting role.

More recently, Bang Kwang has been referenced on the American animated series *American Dad* and the extremely popular *Mafia Wars* online role-playing game. No matter what its reality is, Bang Kwang has earned a place in the world's popular culture and will probably keep it. Like Alcatraz and Sing Sing, Bang Kwang is famous around the world.

Bibliography

Anonymous (n.d.). A Visit to Bang Kwang Central Prison Thailand. Retrieved July 23, 2013, from Stickman's Guide to Bangkok: http://www.stickmanbangkok.com/Reader2006/reader2640.htm

Bangkok Post (2012, May 6). Boozing altruist a "Kindly Killer". Retrieved July 23, 2013, from Bangkok Post: http://www.bangkokpost.com/news/local/292016/boozing-altruist-a-kindly-killer

Bangkwang.net. (2008, September 6). Bangkwang. Retrieved July 23, 2013, from Bangkwang.ent: http://www.bangkwang.net/

BBC News. (2004, July 9). The Real Bangkok Hilton. Retrieved July 23, 2013, from BBC News: http://news.bbc.co.uk/2/hi/programmes/this_world/3899549.stm

Wikipedia (n.d.). Bang Kwang Central Prison. Retrieved July 23, 2013, from Wikipedia: http://en.wikipedia.org/wiki/Bang_Kwang_Central_P rison

Wikipedia (n.d.). Bangkok Hilton. Retrieved July 23, 2013, from Wikipedia: http://en.wikipedia.org/wiki/Bangkok_Hilton

Camp 22 – North Korea

North Korea's Camp 22, or Kwan Li So, is probably the world's worst modern concentration camp. Camp 22 is so infamous that the North Korean government has even published false news stories that say it has been shut down. Satellite images indicate that the notorious North Korean gulag is still very much in operation.

Camp 22 might be every bit as horrendous as the Nazi horror factory known as Auschwitz or the worst of Joseph Stalin's gulags, the difference being that those houses of evil were shut down decades ago while Camp 22 remains in operation.

Stories that come out of Camp 22 are reminiscent of those from Auschwitz, particularly reports of gruesome experiments on human beings. Some of those experiments sound a great deal like the ones conducted by Joseph Mengele and other Nazi doctors at Auschwitz.

Mad Science in North Korea

Camp 22 is located deep in the rugged mountains of North Korea near the Russian and Chinese borders. The Communist dictatorship in North Korea has gone to great lengths to hide its horrors, but news of the evils there has leaked out over the years.

The worst of the reports come from a man named Kwon Hyuk who claims he was once the commandant at Camp 22. In 2004 Hyuk told both the BBC and *The Guardian* newspaper about the kind of mad science practiced by the North Korean government at Camp 22.

Kwon said he saw an entire family—a father, a mother, a son, and a daughter —placed in a gas chamber. A technician then switched on suffocating gas, and scientists, guards, and others watched the family suffocate to death. This sounds like the North Korean government is trying to develop improved versions of the gas chambers used by the Nazis.

Kwon said he thought the gassing was justified because he was told the people were enemies of North Korea. Kwon admitted that he was wrong and that the people were no threat. He later defected to China and changed his name to protect himself from assassination by North Korean thugs.

Poisoned Cabbage

Another frightening experiment was witnessed by a woman named Soon Ok-Lee, who was a prisoner at Camp 22. Soon was ordered to select fifty women prisoners and bring them to a certain point. Like Kwon, she later escaped and made her way to China.

Once there, a guard gave her a basket of cabbage and told her to feed it to the prisoners. Soon followed orders and let the women eat the cabbage. The women started vomiting blood and writhing in pain. Soon said they all died within 20 minutes.

Korean human rights workers believe the experiment was part of the testing of chemical weapons that goes on at Camp 22. The workers note that such testing is official government policy in North Korea, and they have uncovered documents that show people were shipped to Camp 22 for that purpose.

The World's Largest Concentration Camp

The frightening thing is that Camp 22 might contain as many as 50,000 people, or around one quarter of the 200,000 held in the North Korean concentration camp system. These people are in the system for such offenses as ripping up postage stamps with pictures of Kim Il-Sung and his successors on them.

Many other prisoners are Christians that are in the camps because they chose to worship God rather than members of the Kim family. North Koreans are supposed to worship their leader as if he were a god.

The late dictator Kim Jong-Il didn't just punish dissidents; he would imprison three generations of the same family in his camps. Kim Jong-Il's son and successor, Kim Jong-Un, may be continuing these evil practices. Like the Nazi concentration camps, the North Korean gulag contains entire families, including young children, babies, and the elderly.

The North Korean gulag, like everything else in North Korea, is modeled on systems created by Vladimir Lenin and Joseph Stalin in Russia. Those systems in Russia are long gone, but the evil is alive and well in North Korea.

There is also a strong possibility that the North Koreans are deliberately copying the Nazis. News reports have stated that Kim Jong-Un has distributed copies of Hitler's book *Mein Kampf* to his top officials because he likes the ideas contained in it.

The World's Last Concentration Camp

The only good thing about Camp 22 is that it is one of the world's last concentration camps. The other totalitarian regimes that created such camps are now all history. Hopefully Camp 22 will soon join Auschwitz and the gulag as a horror only found in history books.

Perhaps Kim Jong-Un, who has inherited his father's and grandfather's role as dictator of North Korea, will one day face punishment for the evils his family has perpetuated against their own people. Kim himself seems fearful of such punishment. In 2012 he released false news stories that claimed Camp 22 had been shut down. Yet satellite photography indicates that the camp is still open and is being expanded. The pictures showed new buildings, which probably mean that Camp 22 will soon be receiving a new generation of victims for its mad scientists. Hopefully that generation will be the last to face its horrors.

Bibliography

Barnett, A. (2004, January 31). Revealed: the gas chamber of North Korea's gulag. Retrieved July 22, 2013, from The Guardian: http://www.guardian.co.uk/world/2004/feb/01/northkorea

Mizrahi, G. (2012, October 29). Google: Labor Camp 22 is Open for Business. Retrieved July 22, 2013, from The North Korea Blog: http://thenorthkoreablog.com/2012/10/29/google-north-korea-labor-camp-22-open-for-business/

One Free Korea (2012, March). North Korea's Largest Concentration Camps on Google Earth. Retrieved July 22, 2013, from Free Korea: http://freekorea.us/camps/

Sky News (2013, June 19). Kim Jong-Un 'Hands Out Hitler's Mein Kampf'. Retrieved July 22, 2013, from Sky News: http://news.sky.com/story/1105661/kim-jong-un-hands-out-hitlers-mein-kampf

Carandiru Penitentiary, Brazil

Carandiru Penitentiary in Sao Paulo, Brazil, was one of the world's most infamous prisons and an embarrassment to the nation of Brazil. The prison's reputation was so bad that authorities eventually tore it down in an attempt to erase it from history. As usually happens with such attempts to suppress history, it failed.

The prison became infamous as the site of one of the worst prison riots in history and what many critics describe as the worst human rights violation in Brazil's history. The incident, known as the Carandiru Massacre, left 111 inmates dead and still generates political controversy in Brazil.

The massacre was only one incident in the history of Carandiru Penitentiary, which many critics consider one of the world's worst prisons. Carandiru was also the largest prison in Latin America, and in its heyday, it sometimes housed as many as 8,000 inmates at a time.

Sao Paulo's House of Horrors

Part of the reason why it had such a terrible reputation was that Carandiru was built in one of the world's great cities, Sao Paulo, in 1920. The penitentiary had a deceptively modern appearance, but its interior contained conditions that Amnesty International has described as medieval.

Part of the reason why the conditions were so bad was that the guards simply let gangs run the prison. They made little or no effort to maintain order in the cellblocks, nor did they attempt to provide basic services to the inmates.

The prison was so out of control that the chief doctor and other medical staff refused to enter it. Instead, they let prisoners get sick and die. A large percentage of the prisoners were suffering from AIDS, but many others died of conditions that could have been easily treated with antibiotics. One report stated that doctors treating patients didn't even use painkillers.

If that wasn't bad enough, there's evidence that many of the prisoners were not fed or were poorly fed. Some reports indicate that malnutrition was common. The reason for this may have been that gangsters were charging other prisoners for food. Prisoners that couldn't pay couldn't eat.

The Massacre

It is no surprise that such conditions led to a prison riot. In October 1992 prisoners who had had enough finally rose up and seized control of the facility. The guards made no attempt to control the riot; they simply ran off and called in the military police.

Units of the Policia Militar Estado de Sao Paulo, or military police of Sao Paulo State, under the command of the notorious Colonel Ubiratan Guimaraes, were deployed to the prison. Colonel Guimaraes and his men had a very direct method of dealing with rebellious prisoners—they simply shot them down. Reports indicated that the Policia Militar gunned down large numbers of prisoners that tried to surrender.

Around 102 of the 111 inmates who were reportedly killed died from gunshot wounds. Since the prisoners didn't have guns, it can be safely inferred that all of those men were shot by the police. Another nine inmates were stabbed or beaten to death by fellow prisoners.

The incident was so horrific that Colonel Guimaraes was put on trial and convicted. The Colonel was sentenced to 632 years in prison but released when a court declared the verdict a mistrial. The Colonel, a hero to many Brazilians and a villain to many others, was elected to the state legislature then shot and killed in his own apartment in 2006. Guimaraes' murder has never been solved, but it's widely believed he was killed in retaliation for the Carandiru Massacre.

A Nation's Shame

Carandiru Penitentiary remained in business for 10 years after the massacre, but it grew into a national embarrassment. Human rights activists around the world criticized the inhumane conditions and the massacre. Others were outraged at the Brazilian courts' inability to bring Colonel Guimaraes to justice.

Anger at the prison grew when physician Drauzio Varella, who worked at the prison for 12 years, wrote a book about his experiences in 2001. The book was published worldwide and exposed the horrors of Carandiru for all to see. For those who didn't want to read about it, director Hector Babeco made a movie version called *Carandiru*.

Not coincidently, authorities decided to close Carandiru and tear it down in 2002. Authorities did leave part of the prison standing as a museum. The museum features a cellblock and a memorial to those killed in the massacre.

Carandiru Penitentiary is history, but the conditions in Brazil's other prisons are just as bad. In April 2013 Amnesty International examined Brazil's penal system and discovered that overcrowding, inhumane living conditions, disease, lack of medical care, gang violence, torture, and brutality by guards were commonplace. Carandiru is gone, but the horrors that took place there continue all over Brazil.

Bibliography

Amnesty International. (2013, April 15). Carandiru
and the scandal of Brazil's medieval prison system.
Retrieved July 24, 2013, from Amnesty International:
http://www.amnesty.org/en/news/carandiru-and-
scandal-brazil-s-medieval-prison-system-2013-04-15

Prison History (n.d.). Carandiru Prison. Retrieved
July 24, 2013, from Prison History:
http://www.prisonhistory.net/famous-
prisons/carandiru/

Wikipedia (n.d.). Carandiru Massacre. Retrieved July
24, 2013, from Wikipedia:
http://en.wikipedia.org/wiki/Carandiru_massacre

Diyarbakir Prison, Turkey

Diyarbakir has long had a reputation as the home of the toughest and harshest prisons in Turkey. During the 1980s that reputation was taken to new lows by the brutalities practiced in the Martial Law Military Prison set up by Turkey's military dictatorship. The prison itself remains a symbol of contention and conflict that has sparked riots on the streets and public protests.

The town of Diyarbakir in what is now southeastern Turkey was the home to a very harsh prison under the Ottoman Empire in the 19th century. The Sultan used the town's prison to lock up political prisoners, mostly from Eastern Europe, where Christian Slavs opposed Ottoman rule.

In 1980 the Turkish government built a new prison in Diyarbakir that developed a terrible reputation after a coup on Sept. 12, 1980. The Turkish Army overthrew the elected government and realized it needed a place to lock up its enemies. Like the Sultans, the generals turned to Diyarbakir, or rather the new prison just built there.

The Military Law Prison

Under the generals' rule, the Martial Law Military Prison was one of the main locations for imprisoning political enemies. In addition to Turkish Democrats, large numbers of Kurds, an ethnic minority that wanted to carve an independent country from Turkish territory, were imprisoned as well.

Writers, intellectuals, and even members of parliament, which had been abolished, found themselves in the prison. Once there, they were subject to incredible acts of brutality at the hands of guards and officers.

The guards and prisoners gave the tortures inflicted colorful names, which made them all the more insidious. The tortures inflicted in Diyarbakir included "Palestinian hangings," in which prisoners were hung by the arms for hours on end, and "Disco," in which prisoners were made to bathe in sewage.

World of Brutality at Diyarbakir

The allegations of torture and brutality from Diyarbakir are both incredible and frightening, especially with regard to the prisoners' nether regions. One officer, Captain Yildrian, reportedly had a dog that was trained to bite prisoners' genitals. Other guards delighted in attaching electrodes to prisoners' genitals instead. The squeezing and crushing of genitals were also reported.

If that wasn't enough, prisoners were regularly raped and forced to rape each other, sometimes with their relatives watching. To add to the humiliation, naked prisoners were made to climb on top of each other, similar to the American detention facility at Abu Ghraib in Iraq. Another method of humiliation was to make prisoners urinate on each other.

There were also reports that guards deliberately pulled the fingernails out of prisoners. Yet another terror was mock executions, in which prisoners were told they'd be killed but then they were not.

The terror was reinforced by the fact that dozens of prisoners died in Diyarbakir, most of them from injuries inflicted by the guards. It is hard to know how many were really killed because the guards would use euphemisms, such as "killed in a hunger strike" or "suicide," to cover up their abuses.

Riot and Trial

Diyarbakir became a symbol of evil in Turkey, particularly to the Kurds. The prison remained in business by holding political prisoners, even after the military government stepped down and democracy returned. The government kept it open in order to use it against the Kurds.

The prison became a political liability for Turkey and a media sensation on Sept. 24, 1996, when a riot broke out there. During the riot, police and commandos stormed the prison and killed at least 10 prisoners.

The riot led to investigations by the public prosecutor, the Human Rights Commission of the Turkish Parliament, and the European Court of Human Rights. The court had jurisdiction because Turkey was trying to join the European Union. The Parliamentary Commission determined that 29 soldiers and 38 police officers had violated the law during the riot.

A trial was eventually held and up to 72 people were indicted. The trial dragged on until 2006. Eventually, 62 individuals were sentenced to 18 years in prison, but most only served six years for various reasons. A higher court later quashed many of the sentences.

Symbol of Evil

In recent years there have been attempts to close Diyarbakir. The Turkish government wants to turn it into a school, while Kurdish activists want to turn the building into a museum to honor those who died. Bizarrely enough, there were even street protests and riots over the prison staged by Kurdish activists, who were angry at plans to turn the prison into a school.

Diyarbakir is still up and running, but it is apparently a normal prison for regular criminals today. Efforts by activists to turn it into a museum of shame have stalled. So, apparently, have the plans to convert the facility into a school.

Legal battles continue as well as political ones. Recent news stories indicate that hundreds of people in Turkey have filed charges against former Diyarbakir guards, whom they blame for human rights abuses. It isn't clear if these charges are legal, but they will probably drag on for years to come. Diyarbakir is a symbol of evil that doesn't seem to go away, even though the Turkish government would like it to disappear.

Bibliography

Kajeski, J. (2011, December 30). Turkey's Museum of Shame. Retrieved July 24, 2013, from Pulitzer Center on Crisis Reporting: http://pulitzercenter.org/reporting/turkey-diyarbakir-prison-pkk-kurdish-activists-torture-repression-museum-shame-erdogan

Wikipedia (n.d.). Diyarbakir Prison. Retrieved July 24, 2013, from Wikipedia: http://en.wikipedia.org/wiki/Diyarbak%C4%B1r_Prison

Zana, M. (1998, June 26). What I Witnessed in Diyarbakir Prison. Retrieved July 24, 2013, from American Kurdish Information Network: http://kurdistan.org/work/speeches/what-i-witnessed-in-diyarbakir-prison/

Drapchi Prison

Drapchi Prison in Tibet's capital, Lhasa, has some of the strangest prisoners in the world—large numbers of Buddhist monks and nuns. The nuns and monks are imprisoned there because they oppose China's occupation of Tibet. In Tibet, peaceful men and women of faith are often treated as criminals and placed in prison.

Drapchi Prison, or Lhasa Prison No. 1 as it is officially known, was reportedly built as a military garrison by the independent Tibetan government. It was converted into a prison in 1965 during Mao Zedong's infamous Cultural Revolution, when the dictator had his Red Guard thugs smash all vestiges of traditional culture. Tibetans, who preferred their traditional Buddhist faith to Mao's personality cult, were a major target of the Red Guards.

Today, Drapchi is considered a symbol of Chinese oppression of the Tibetan people. It houses large numbers of people whose only crime is to want to live in a free and independent country. Many of the prisoners are devout Tibetan Buddhists that believe the Chinese are waging ethnic cleansing against their people.

Inhumane Treatment and the Singing Nuns

The most famous prisoners at Drapchi were the singing nuns of the 1990s. Their crime was to sing a song condemning the prison and celebrating Tibet's spiritual leader, the Dalai Lama. The Lama was forced to flee Tibet in 1959 when a CIA-backed revolt against Chinese rule in Tibet collapsed. The Lama currently heads up a Tibetan government in exile in India that opposes Chinese occupation of Tibet.

The nuns were young women imprisoned in 1993 for taking part in peaceful demonstrations against the Chinese occupation. In prison they recorded a series of songs that condemned the inhumanity and brutality of the Chinese gulag. For that crime they were sentenced to several additional years in Drapchi.

Five of the nuns later died from the abuse they received in Drapchi. Six others were released and made their way to free countries such as India, Switzerland, and the United States. Seven other nuns reportedly remain in Tibet, and it is not known if they have been arrested again or not.

Tapes of the nuns' songs were smuggled out and circulated throughout Tibet. The nuns have held reunion concerts in cities like London in order to raise awareness of the plight of the Tibetan people.

Food Used as a Weapon

Prisoners in Drapchi, who include 164 women and elderly monks as old as 84, regularly endure beatings and torture. They also face malnutrition, which is used as a deliberate means of control and torture rather than a result of food shortages.

The authorities at Drapchi deliberately withhold food from prisoners in an attempt to control them. This is a classic method of torture that was used extensively by Joseph Stalin and other Communist dictators.

Conditions in Drapchi are so harsh that some of the survivors suffer from anxiety and panic attacks created by the memory of their time there. Just the memory of Drapchi can cause such anxiety.

Hunger Strikes

Inmates at Drapchi have occasionally revolted against the Chinese. In 1996 all of the inmates in Drapchi's Unit 3 reportedly went on strike against the prison administration. The authorities at the camp may have caved into their demands because they didn't want the bad publicity from the deaths of inmates.

The strike, like the singing nuns' incident, raised awareness of the camp and its inmates. Despite the incidents, it is believed that Drapchi is still very much in business and will remain so in the future.

Still in Business

The latest reports indicate that Drapchi is still used as a prison, and it has recently been expanded. The camp reportedly contains 1,000 prisoners, but it might hold more in the future.

Around 600 of the inmates are political prisoners, but at least 400 others might be housed there. The camp's administrators might be using a technique borrowed from the Soviet gulag in which criminals were used to terrorize and control political prisoners.

The presence of criminals also allows the government to maintain the fiction that Drapchi is a prison and its inmates are criminals. It isn't clear if anybody actually believes such lies, but such deception is standard practice for Communist regimes like that in China.

Drapchi the Musical

Strangely enough, Drapchi was the subject of a musical movie released in 2012. *Drapchi* tells the story of a Tibetan opera singer imprisoned in the gulag and spotlights some of the experiences of the singing nuns. The movie was shot partly and secretly in Lhasa and was shown at film festivals in Europe in 2012.

Even though the movie is a wrap, the story of Drapchi is far from over. The prison remains in business and will probably remain so as long as the Chinese Army occupies Tibet.

Bibliography

Drapchi 14 Reunion (n.d.). Echoes of Drapchi Prison. Retrieved July 22, 2013, from Drapchi 14 Reunion: http://www.drapchi14reunion.com/index.html

Wikipedia (n.d.). Drapchi (Film). Retrieved July 22, 2013, from Wikipedia: http://en.wikipedia.org/wiki/Drapchi_(film)

Wikipedia (n.d.). Drapchi Prison. Retrieved July 22, 2013, from Wikipedia: http://en.wikipedia.org/wiki/Drapchi_Prison

Gldani Prison

The prison systems in the various republics that make up the former Soviet Union have a reputation for brutality and corruption. One prison, Gldani, which is in the Republic of Georgia, has attracted special attention because of videos of guards abusing prisoners.

Conditions in Gldani were so bad that they prompted protests, an investigation by the European Union, and a political scandal. The political scandal actually led to popular outrage that brought down the Georgian government and affected the outcome of elections. The reports also raised questions about the reforms in Georgia and the small country's attempts at democratic reforms.

The uproar over Gldani was reminiscent of the Abu Ghraib scandal in the United States and Iraq because it involved the humiliation and sexual abuse of prisoners by guards. As at Abu Ghraib, there were pictures and even videotape of the abuse that appeared in the media to generate a frenzy.

A Country in Turmoil

Georgia is a small country that has suffered a lot in its history. It has been conquered by the Turks and the Russians, and the Soviets deprived it of independence and the Georgian people of their freedom.

Georgia finally regained its independence when the Soviet Union collapsed in 1991, but since then, it hasn't had an easy time of it. There have been constant allegations of corruption in the country and a longstanding conflict with Russia that has erupted into war on at least one occasion.

Yet the Gldani abuse scandal touched a special nerve in the Georgian people, perhaps because they suffered so much under Communism. The scandal came just as much of the population was fed up with their longtime leader, Mikhail Saakashvili.

Torture on Video Tape

The Georgian people learned of the abuse at Gldani Prison, which is outside of the capital of Tbilisi, in the worst possible way. On Sept. 18, 2012, graphic video of guards abusing prisoners was broadcast on the nightly news.

The videos were reportedly secretly taped in the prison by an unknown individual. One video that really outraged Georgians showed a man being stripped naked and spat upon by prison guards. An even more horrific video showed a masked man being stripped, humiliated, and raped.

In the videos, prisoners were asked if they were thieves-in-law. A thief-in-law is a Russian or Georgian term for gangster. The guards wanted to know if the prisoners were members of a mob. They also forced prisoners to denounce thieves-in-law or organized crime on the tapes. The guards may have been planning to play the tapes for the gangsters in prison who would presumably beat up or kill the prisoners insulting the mob.

Political Firestorm in Georgia

The airing of the videos on Georgian television ignited a political firestorm that brought down the country's government. The Prime Minister resigned, and large numbers of protestors took to the streets.

Even Saakashvili claimed to be horrified by the tapes, which he called inhumane. That didn't stop the country's Interior Minister from claiming that an inmate was paid to make the video by unknown individuals in an attempt to discredit the government.

The tapes surfaced just two weeks before parliamentary elections. Saakashvili and his supporters blamed their main opponent, shadowy billionaire Bidzina Ivanishvili, for the tapes. The prosecutor's office, which was controlled by the President, stated publicly that two of Ivanishvili's supporters were responsible for the tape.

The Controversy Continues

The videotape did prompt one response that would have never happened in Soviet times. The guards pictured in the videotape were arrested and are now facing trial for abusing prisoners.

The nation's Prime Minister was also forced to resign as a result of the scandal. The video showed that Georgia is a democracy and that its government is responsible to the people.

The firestorm over the Gldani tapes is far from over in Georgia. The nation's Minister of Interior Affairs has told the press that he wants order during the presidential elections scheduled for October 2013. Many observers believe the elections will lead to violence.

Saakashvili's followers, the United National Movement, have accused the Georgian Dream, the ruling party, of organizing riots. They also accuse Georgian Dream of using events like the Gldani tape to manipulate public opinion.

It is likely that more tapes of abuse in Georgia's prisons will surface and find their way onto television as the election approaches. The Gldani tapes allowed Bidzina Ivanishvili's Georgia Dream party to win the parliamentary election last fall. It isn't hard to imagine the coalition using the same technique again. In Georgia, prison abuse makes for good politics, even if it is horrifying.

Bibliography

Associated Press. (2012, September 12). Georgia protestors call for prosecutions over prison abuse. Retrieved July 26, 2013, from The Guardian: http://www.guardian.co.uk/world/2012/sep/21/georgia-protesters-demand-prison-prosecutions

Elder, M. (2012, September 19). Georgia prison guards 'captured on video torturing prisoner'. Retrieved July 26, 2013, from The Guardian: http://www.guardian.co.uk/world/2012/sep/19/georgia-prison-guards-torture-video

Gadimova, N. (2013, July 27). Georgia's interior ministry urges public order during pre-election events. Retrieved July 26, 2013, from Azernews: http://www.azernews.az/region/57325.html

Human Rights Watch (2012, September 19). Georgia: Investigates Sexual Abuse in Prison. Retrieved July 26, 2013, from Human Rights Watch: http://www.hrw.org/news/2012/09/19/georgia-investigate-sexual-abuse-prison

RTT Staff Writer (2012, September 20). EU 'Appalled' By Georgia Prisoner Video. Retrieved July 26, 2013, from RTT News: http://www.rttnews.com/1969509/eu-appalled-by-georgia-prisoner-abuse-video.aspx

Wikipedia (n.d.). Gldani prison scandal. Retrieved July 26, 2013, from Wikipedia: http://en.wikipedia.org/wiki/Gldani_prison_scandal

Guantanamo Bay

The top secret U.S. military detention facility at Guantanamo Bay, Cuba, is probably the most controversial prison in history. Nobody can agree on whether it should exist or even if the United States has a legal right to hold those detained.

President Obama wants to shut it down, but he cannot do so because of the political controversy. Republicans in the U.S. Congress want to keep Guantanamo Bay open because they think it is necessary for national security. Their argument is that there is nowhere to else to imprison captured terrorists and no other means of preventing them from attacking the United States in the future.

The controversy over Guantanamo Bay was greatly aggravated when it was revealed that some of the prisoners there had been tortured. The torture included such methods as the water treatment (or water boarding) and sleep deprivation, which are banned by the United States Constitution.

What to Do with the Terrorists?

Guantanamo Bay became a prison because of an interesting dilemma the United States had during the early days of the War on Terror. U.S. forces captured large numbers of terrorists, including members of Al Qaeda, but didn't know what to do with them. Part of the problem was that the terrorists were at war with the United States, but they were not part of any recognized military force or fighting for a nation.

Nobody knew what to do with the fighters; they had taken arms against the United States, but they were citizens of countries America was not at war with, and to make matters worse, some of them were citizens of U.S. allies. They couldn't be held in the United States, because they were not prisoners and most of them had committed no crimes on American soil.

Authorities didn't want to bring the terrorists to the United States where they would be under the jurisdiction of U.S. courts. In particular, they didn't want them released on U.S. soil where they could apply for asylum or commit more atrocities. There had to be someplace else to send them, and that's when somebody remembered the naval base at Guantanamo Bay, Cuba.

Legal Limbo in Cuba

Guantanamo Bay is the oldest United States naval facility outside of U.S. territory. The base sits on the largest bay on the southern side of Cuba. The U.S. took possession of the base under the Cuban-American Treaty of 1903 after the Spanish-American War.

The problem is that the Communist dictatorship of Fidel Castro, which is the current legal government of Cuba, does not recognize the Cuban-American Treaty. The Castro regime insists the treaty was obtained by force and violates international law, so it is not binding. That would theoretically make Guantanamo Bay Cuban territory, but Cuba lacks the military force to seize it from the United States.

Since it was legally not in the United States, Guantanamo Bay was the perfect place to hold the captured terrorists because they would not be subject to U.S. law. Theoretically, they would be subject to Cuban law, but since the current Cuban constitution is nothing but an imitation of the Soviet one, nobody has raised that point. Part of the reason why Guantanamo Bay is a perfect prison is that Fidel Castro deliberately isolated it from the rest of Cuba. He cut off the base and surrounded it with troops and mines to keep his people from defecting to the U.S. and embarrassing his regime.

Who Is at Guantanamo?

The first prisoners were shipped to Guantanamo Bay
in January 2002. Contrary to popular belief, no
prisoners have been shipped there since 2008. Almost
all of those at the base were members of Al Qaeda
captured in Afghanistan. No prisoners captured in
Iraq were shipped there.

The *New York Times* estimates that 770 prisoners
have been held at Guantanamo at one time or another.
All of them were men, and most of them (604) have
been released or sent back to their homelands. The
largest number of prisoners were from Afghanistan
and Saudi Arabia, but citizens of Egypt, Algeria,
Yemen, Pakistan, the United Kingdom, and even
Australia were held there at various times. A few
prisoners died by committing suicide.

Most of the prisoners released from Guantanamo are living normal lives in their home countries. A small number have returned to terrorism, and a few have been killed in U.S. military attacks. The problem is that there are around 160 prisoners at Guantanamo Bay that cannot be returned to their own nations. Their governments refuse to take them back for a variety of reasons. There are also some individuals that U.S. authorities believe might be a threat if they are ever released.

The Problem That Won't Go Away

The big problem at Guantanamo was that nobody knew what do with the prisoners. President George W. Bush originally wanted the prisoners tried by military tribunals, but the U.S. Supreme Court ruled that that was illegal. President Obama suggested trying them in U.S. courts, but that was another proposal that fell flat.

Obama ordered Guantanamo closed in January 2009 shortly after his election, but it is still open. The President is still committed to closing the detention facility, but he hasn't been able to because of congressional opposition. Republicans in Congress have effectively been able to keep the prison open.

In 2013 the prisoners there made news again by staging a hunger strike. Around 100 of the inmates were supposedly involved in the strike. It isn't clear whether the strike will lead to the camp's shutdown or not.

Life in Guantanamo

Ironically enough, the conditions that detainees stay in at Guantanamo are not that bad. They live in air conditioned buildings similar to army barracks, have plenty of food, and have access to the Internet, satellite TV, and even Skype. The inmates even have a soccer field. Observers have said conditions are better there than those in most federal prisons in the United States. All of the inmates are allowed to practice their Islamic faith freely and have access to the Koran.

Only troublemakers are held in solitary confinement, which is similar to a regular federal prison cell. Most of the prisoners are still in the barracks, although authorities have recently cracked down on some of them.

A Comfortable Legal Limbo

In the past, some Guantanamo inmates may have been subject to questionable interrogation techniques, such as the water treatments that are considered torture by many critics. That means simulated drowning is used to force a person to reveal information. Cynics maintained that the U.S. housed the prisoners at Guantanamo specifically so they would not be under the protections of the U.S. Constitution. Since then, U.S. Supreme Court rulings have determined that the prisoners are under U.S. law and enjoy Constitutional protections.

This means that the prisoners are still in a sort of legal limbo. The U.S. courts have ruled that their incarceration is unconstitutional, but they are still in prison. Despite Obama's promises to close the facility, no serious effort to return the remaining prisoners to their homelands has been made.

Such interrogation is no longer used, and most inmates spend their time watching TV, reading, or playing soccer. The prisoners have no hope of release, but their current situation is very comfortable. Many of them are enjoying a far better lifestyle at the American taxpayers' expense than they would back home.

The future of Guantanamo Bay and its prisoners is still very much up in the air. President Obama would like to close the facility, possibly so he can negotiate a new treaty about the base's future with Cuba, yet it's likely that Guantanamo Bay will remain open for the foreseeable future. It's one problem that seems to never go away.

Bibliography

Golden, T. (2006, September 17). The Battle for Guantanamo. Retrieved July 23, 2013, from New York Times: http://www.nytimes.com/2006/09/17/magazine/17gua ntanamo.html?ref=guantanamobaynavalbasecuba&_r =0

Greenberg, K. (2013, May 7). The top five myths about Guantanamo Bay. Retrieved July 23, 2013, from Raw Story: http://www.rawstory.com/rs/2013/05/07/the-top-five-myths-about-guantanamo-bay/

Serrano, R. A. (2013, June 17). Envoy appointed to shut down prison at Guantanamo. Retrieved July 23, 2013, from Los Angeles Times: http://articles.latimes.com/2013/jun/17/nation/la-na-obama-guantanamo-20130618

The New York Times/National Public Radio. (2012, December 11). The Guantanamo Docket. Retrieved July 23, 2013, from The New York Times: http://projects.nytimes.com/guantanamo?ref=guantan amobaynavalbasecuba

Wikipedia. (n.d.). Guantanamo Bay. Retrieved July 23, 2013, from Wikipedia: http://en.wikipedia.org/wiki/Guant%C3%A1namo_Bay

La Sante Prison

La Sante Prison, in the heart of Paris, is one of the oldest prisons still in use in any industrialized country. It is also one of the most notorious and inhumane. The prison, built in 1867 by the Emperor Napoleon III, is still in use and is notoriously overcrowded.

Since it is right in the heart of the French capital, La Sante has played host to a number of celebrity inmates. Famous prisoners have included former Panamanian dictator and drug smuggler Manuel Noriega, notorious terrorist Carlos the Jackal, and Japanese cannibal Isse Sagawa.

When it opened in 1867, La Sante was a model institution, but in recent decades it has become notorious for inhumane conditions. During the 1990s the facility's former doctor, Veronique Vasseur, noted that prisoners shared their cells with rats and fleas. She also noted that drug dealing, gang warfare, and suicide were common in the prison. La Sante is still open for business and has the distinction of being one of the last prisons located in the capital of a major power.

A Historic Location

Not only is La Sante one of the world's oldest working prisons, but it is also one of the most historic. One of the last executions in France took place in the facility in 1972 when murderers Roger Bontems and Claude Buffet died on the guillotine.

One of the most notable features of La Sante was a special courtyard with a guillotine so executions could take place in the heart of the French capital. The guillotine is no longer used because France abolished the death penalty in 1981. Many prisoners waiting for transport to the notorious penal colony on Devil's Island were also housed at La Sante.

Used by the Nazis

During World War II, La Sante, the Nazis, and the French Vichy government that collaborated with the Germans, imprisoned members of the French Resistance there. Around 18 French patriots were murdered by collaborators at the prison. There was a famous revolt in the prison on Bastille Day in 1944, when American, British, and Canadian armies were approaching Paris. During the revolt, Vichy soldiers gunned down fellow Frenchmen on the day the French were supposed to celebrate their "Liberte."

Many other French prisoners died when the Nazis shipped them from La Sante to the concentration camps in Germany and Poland. It isn't known if Jews were housed in La Sante, but they may have been.

National Shame and Outrage

As France entered the 21st century, La Sante became the center of a national scandal. Dr. Vasseur published a book describing her experiences as the prison doctor and exposed the horrific conditions in the facility.

She noted that La Sante had become terribly overcrowded and had not been modernized. Part of the reason why the prison was so crowded was that there is no parole in France; French courts have the right to keep people imprisoned for months or weeks on end as they wait for trial. That means innocent people can be imprisoned with hardened convicts.

Vasseur noted that these people were often raped and terrorized by the criminals kept in La Sante. The prison was further crowded by large numbers of drug offenders that were locked up at the time. In 2000 nearly half of the 55,000 people in French prisons had never been convicted of a crime.

Hellish Prisons

Another telling sign was that the suicide rate in French prisons was several times higher than any other nation. In 1999, 124 prisoners committed suicide in French prisons, while only 24 inmates killed themselves in the California State Prison system, which housed 160,000 prisoners.

The reason for this is that French prisons, including La Sante, are notoriously hellish. Prisoners are regularly locked in dungeon-type cells that haven't been modernized since the 19th century. In 2008 a prisoner named Christian Donat successfully sued the nation's Ministry of Justice over conditions in his cell in Rouen. The court awarded Donat $4,700 in damages after it found that his cell violated health regulations.

Despite such complaints and lawsuits, little seems to have been done to improve French prisons. Human rights activists noted that some French prison cells were smaller than the recommended size for a dog kennel.

Renovation or White Washed

Like many buildings in Paris, La Sante is currently being renovated, at least on the outside. Recent news articles indicate that the building will soon have glass cupolas and covered green spaces. The prison will remain open, but the prison will be modernized. Some of the plans call for better restaurants and conditions that are more in line with other European prisons.

It isn't clear if any of the renovations will benefit the prisoners. One of the architects who submitted a plan for the project would like to help the prisoners. News reports indicate that the architect, Pierre Botton, served time for embezzlement in La Sante in the 1990s. His plans call for greenhouses, a glass roof, and a restaurant open to the public to be added to the prison. The restaurant would presumably be staffed by prisoners that would cook the food and serve the patrons. The plan reportedly caught the attention of former French President Nicolas Sarkozy.

If Botton's plans are followed through, Paris's most notorious prison could become a tourist attraction. The media reports don't say if his suggestion was taken or not, despite the presidential interest.

Bibliography

ANSAmed. (2012, March 2). France: 2014 renovation of historic Paris prison La Sante. Retrieved July 25, 2013, from ANSA med: http://www.ansamed.info/ansamed/en/news/nations/france/2012/03/02/visualizza_new.html_126393999.html

Curtis, B. (2010, June). Inside the Prison De La Sante - An Eyewitness Account. Retrieved July 25, 2013, from Invisible Paris: http://parisisinvisible.blogspot.com/2010/06/inside-prison-de-la-sante-eyewitness.html

Daley, S. (2000, January 28). Expose of Brutal Prison Jolts France's Self-Image. Retrieved July 14, 2013, from New York Times: http://www.nytimes.com/2000/01/28/world/expose-of-brutal-prison-jolts-france-s-self-image.html

Vicusi, G. (2008, July 31). Rats, Disease Plague Prisoners in France's Overcrowded Jails. Retrieved July 24, 2013, from Bloomberg: http://www.bloomberg.com/apps/news?pid=newsarchive&sid=a2jxTjq6EHVc

Wikipedia (n.d.). La Sante Prison. Retrieved July 25, 2013, from Wikipedia: http://en.wikipedia.org/wiki/La_Sant%C3%A9_Priso n

Maracaibo Prison

Maracaibo National Jail in Venezuela is notorious as one of the world's most violent and dangerous prisons, so it's not surprising that the jail was the location of one of the most violent prison riots in history. The riot led to the grisly deaths of as many as 106 prisoners.

Maracaibo wasn't the deadliest documented prison riot in history because 111 prisoners died in a riot at Brazil's Carandiru Penitentiary in 1992. Since most of the deaths at Carandiru were caused by soldiers that stormed the prison to put down the riot, Maracaibo might be a worse riot. Most of the deaths at Maracaibo were caused by the riot itself rather than authorities.

Some reports put the death toll from the Maracaibo riot at 130. If those figures are correct, that would make Maracaibo the deadliest prison riot in recent history. The Venezuelan government has refused to make the real figures available, so it is impossible to tell which riot was the most destructive.

The riot was an incredibly brutal one because of the violence the inmates inflicted on each other. Part of the reason why the rioting was so bad was that it was driven by racism. The Maracaibo uprising was essentially a race riot behind bars, complete with lynching and ethnic violence.

Race Riot Behind Bars

The riot was provoked by a brutal murder in early January 1994. White prisoners in Maracaibo beheaded a prisoner that was a member of the Guajiro Indian tribe. When they heard about the murder, the Guajiro prisoners in the overcrowded facility went on the rampage with a simple objective: kill all the non-Indian prisoners.

Several hundred Guajiros stormed into the cellblocks controlled by white and black prisoners. Once in the cellblocks, the mob started stabbing, shooting, beating, and drowning any non-Indian prisoner they could find. Many reports said some of the Guajiros were armed with machetes that they used to chop other prisoners to pieces.

Witnesses said many of the rioters mutilated white prisoners and cut off their heads. They also tore up the bodies of non-Indian prisoners. Lt. Colonel Aldo Boccone, a National Guard officer whose unit was called in to put down the riot, said he believed the riot was a planned act of vengeance for the earlier killing.

Inferno Behind Bars

To add to the carnage, the rioters started tossing Molotov cocktails into the cells where prisoners were trapped. A Molotov cocktail is a homemade bomb consisting of a bottle filled with a flammable liquid and a wick, usually a piece of cloth. The cloth is lit and the bottle is tossed; when it lands and breaks apart, the effect is similar to that of an incendiary grenade.

The homemade fire bombs started a series of blazes that quickly turned into an inferno. The cellblock became an incinerator that saw at least 54 prisoners burned alive. Since many of them were in their cells, some of the prisoners may have been doused with flammable liquids or burning liquids by their attackers.

The prisoners in the burning cellblocks faced a horrible choice. They could try to flee and get chopped up by the lynch mob or burn to death in their cells. The scope of the fire indicates that the rioters planned to set the cellblocks on fire with the prisoners in them.

At least one prisoner, Daniel Paz, escaped from the inferno by jumping 30 feet from his cellblock. Other prisoners probably died jumping from the cellblocks to escape the flames.

The Military Moves In

The only thing that stopped the rampage and more deaths was the Venezuelan National Guard, which moved in about five hours after the riot. The Guard filled the prison with tear gas and probably shot more than a few prisoners dead.

The situation in the jail was so bad that 250 National Guardsmen remained on duty outside the prison for several days. The only way authorities could control the prison was with the help of heavily armed soldiers.

The riot was only the last incident in a cycle of violence that had been gripping the prison for years. Maracaibo had a reputation for violence and brutality long before the riot erupted.

The World's Most Violent Prison

In the year before the riot, 48 prisoners were murdered in Maracaibo National Jail. Many of the prisoners died in gang fights and ethnic bloodshed between Indian and non-Indian inmates.

In addition to being violent, the jail was terribly overcrowded. It had been built to house 1,500 inmates but was holding 2,500 prisoners at the time of the uprising. Around 800 of the prisoners were Guajiros, who like most Indians in South America, are poor and oppressed.

The prisoners had more to be angry about than racially motivated violence. Press reports indicated that most of the prisoners in Venezuelan prisons had never been tried or convicted of a crime. They had to wait years to see a courtroom, which obviously increased the frustration and tensions behind bars.

The World's Most Violent Prison System

Maracaibo was typical of Venezuelan prisons that had a reputation as the most violent and brutal in Latin America. On the same day as the riot, Jan. 5, 1994, National Guardsmen shot 10 escaping prisoners from another prison in Maracay, Venezuela.

Venezuela's prisons have not changed much in the 20 years since the Maracaibo riot. In June 2011, 25 prisoners were killed in a riot at the El Rodeo prison near Caracas. After that incident, *Time* magazine reported that prison gangs had taken control of El Rodeo and convicts armed with AK-47 assault rifles were patrolling the cellblocks.

Some of the gangs added a modern twist to the violence by posting videos of prisoners beheading and disemboweling other inmates on YouTube. The El Rodeo riot included a nine-hour shootout between rival prison gangs.

Venezuela still has the world's most violent and dangerous prison system. Prisoners there are more likely to get killed by their fellow inmates than almost anywhere else in the world.

Bibliography

Gupta, G. (2011, June 23). Venezuela's Horrific Prison Riot: Why is Hugo Chavez Silent? Retrieved July 28, 2013, from Time: http://www.time.com/time/world/article/0,8599,2079 611,00.html

New York Times (1994, January 5). Ethnic Feud in Venezuela Jail Kills 106. Retrieved July 28, 2013, from New York Times: http://www.nytimes.com/1994/01/05/world/ethnic-feud-in-venezuela-jail-kills-106.html

Pelican Bay

The California State Prison at Pelican Bay is so harsh that prisoners there went on a hunger strike to protest their conditions in July 2013. The prisoners on strike were in the Security Housing Unit, the State of California's answer to Supermax. The Security Housing Unit is the toughest prison in California; the prisoners in it are kept under permanent lockdown.

California has so many prisoners in its prison system that the state has its own Supermax at Pelican Bay near Crescent City, along the state's north coast. Pelican Bay houses the toughest and most violent prisoners in California's system. That includes many members of America's worst prison gangs, such as the Mexican Mafia.

The only way to get into Pelican Bay's Supermax facility is to commit a crime in another prison. Most of the prisoners are there because the guards at other prisons cannot control them. Critics have pointed out that many of the prisoners in Pelican Bay are there because they broke prison rules and not because they committed crimes against citizens.

Two Prisons in One

Pelican Bay actually consists of two prisons: a fairly normal maximum security facility and the Security Housing Unit also known as the SHU. It is the SHU that serves as California's Supermax. The prison is so harsh that it has drawn criticism from human rights activists and others.

Prisoners in the SHU are confined for 22 hours alone in a small cell every day, and many of them can only leave it if they are in chains. The conditions at Pelican Bay are much like those at the notorious Russian prison on Petak Island and the federal ADX Supermax near Florence, Colo. As at Petak Island and Supermax, the SHU prisoners are kept under permanent lockdown.

The cells in the SHU have no windows, and prisoners don't go to a cafeteria to eat. Instead, food is given to prisoners through a slot in the door. Once a day prisoners are allowed to exercise in a very small area called the "dog run." The dog run is a small outdoor courtyard the size of three cells. It is called the dog run because it is similar to the spaces used to exercise dogs in veterinary clinics. The only other times prisoners can leave cells are to see their lawyers or visitors or to take a shower.

Some critics have alleged that conditions at Pelican Bay's SHU are so harsh they drive men insane. Similar complaints have been made about Petak Island.

Controversy and Anger

In a strange twist of fate, it isn't the harsh conditions that draw the most anger from Pelican Bay SHU prisoners. Instead, the biggest frustration is with the system used to determine which prisoners go into the SHU and which don't.

The system is called debriefing, but prisoners call it snitching. The big complaint is that prisoners can only get out of the SHU by ratting out a fellow prisoner. If the prisoner has no information about his fellow prisoners, he has to stay. Since prisoners are kept in isolation, they often know little or nothing about their fellow inmates.

Other factors that can keep a prisoner in SHU include gang affiliations and rule violations. To get out of the SHU, a prisoner must be reassessed by guards. Critics of the system, such as law professor Julius Lobel, claim that guards abuse this system to keep prisoners they don't like in the security unit.

The Living Tomb

Critics have also claimed that prisoners are given rotten food and denied medical care. Another big reason why prisoners hate the SHU is that they don't get some of the normal privileges most American inmates take for granted, such as telephone calls and regular visits from their families.

Lobel has labeled the SHU a human rights abuse and said a prisoner told him the unit is a "living tomb." The unit earned this reputation because it is built entirely of concrete and units are completely undecorated. Another common complaint about the facility is that it is poorly ventilated so it gets extremely hot in the summer and cold in the winter.

Another reason why Pelican Bay generates so much controversy is that most of the prisoners in it were not sentenced to it by a court. Instead, they were sent there by prison authorities because they violated prison rules.

Hunger Strike

Pelican Bay has generated something very unusual for an American prison: a hunger strike. In July 2013 a disputed number of prisoners in the facility stopped eating in an attempt to force authorities to give them better treatment. Some reports indicated that as many as 100 prisoners were striking.

This was the second strike at Pelican Bay; there was a similar strike in July 2011. The prisoners in the strike contended that they had no choice because prison authorities had refused to improve their conditions.

There are also a number of lawsuits directed at the methods used in the Security Unit. The attorneys for the prisoners claim that the SHU constitutes cruel and unusual punishment, which violates the U.S. Constitution. Another complaint is that the procedures used to send prisoners there violate the Constitution's guarantee of due process.

Pelican Bay isn't just one of America's toughest prisons; it is also one of America's most controversial. The controversy swirling around Pelican Bay will not end anytime soon.

Bibliography

Lobel, J. (2013, July 15). Jules Lobel: Pelican Bay prisoners trapped in inhumane conditions. Retrieved July 27, 2013, from San Jose Mercury News: http://www.mercurynews.com/ci_23650999/jules-lobel-pelican-bay-prisoners-trapped-inhumane-conditions

Montgomery, M. (2013, July 25). Calif. Inmates 'Prepared to Starve Themselves' to Protest Indefinite Isolation. Retrieved July 27, 2013, from PBS Newshour: http://www.pbs.org/newshour/bb/nation/july-dec13/hungerstrike_07-25.html

Wikipedia (n.d.). Pelican Bay State Prison. Retrieved July 27, 2013, from Wikipedia: http://en.wikipedia.org/wiki/Pelican_Bay_State_Prison

Petak Island Prison, Russia

Petak Island is known as the Alcatraz of Russia. Like Alcatraz, Petak Island has a reputation as being an escape-proof prison where only the worst criminals are sent. It also has a reputation for harsh conditions similar to those in Supermax and Pelican Bay in the United States.

This remote facility, located far to the north of Moscow, has the reputation of being Russia's toughest prison. That's saying a lot in a country long known for having some of the world's harshest penal institutions and toughest criminals. It's also the home to Russia's death row, although nobody has been executed in the country in over a decade. There's a moratorium on executions in Russia.

The Supermax of Russia

Petak Island has a lot in common with Supermax. Like Supermax, the prisoners are all kept in lockdown most of the time, around 22 hours a day. As at Supermax and Pelican Bay, prisoners have to eat in their cells.

There is one big difference between Supermax and Petak Island. Petak Island inmates have to share their cells with another prisoner. Each small cell is designed to house two convicts. The cells have no bathroom facilities, and human rights advocates estimate that half the prison's population is suffering from tuberculosis and other serious diseases.

Only prisoners that are being punished get to spend time alone. They are sent to a dungeon-like cell with nothing but a bed and a metal bucket to be used as a toilet. Prisoners in solitary at Petak Island must stand all day and are not allowed to read or leave the cell.

The regime there is more like that at a top U.S. prison than a traditional Russian facility. Unlike most Russian prisons, the guards are firmly in control on Petak Island. Most Russian prisons are run by vicious prison gangs known as the Thieves' World. The Thieves' World is so powerful that many Russian prison wardens actually take orders from it.

The Alcatraz of Russia

Petak Island has something else in common with Supermax—nobody has ever escaped from it. Yet it isn't the harsh discipline that keeps the prisoners inside Petak Island; instead, it's the facility's location.

Like Alcatraz, Petak is built on an island, but the difference is that the island is in the middle of a lake rather than a bay. The only way on and off the island is over two rickety bridges or by boat. Prisoners that made it over the wall would have to swim through the cold water.

They would also have to get by the guards on the towers. The guards have orders to shoot any prisoner that tries to run, and they will. So far, no prisoner has successfully made it out of Petak Island. It isn't known how many prisoners have died trying to escape from there.

A Prison That Drives Men Insane

Petak Island is so tough that it can drive some of the world's hardest criminals insane. The prison's psychologist, Svetlana Kiseylova, told the British newspaper *The Telegraph* that Petak destroys people. After three or four years in the facility, most prisoners' personalities are destroyed.

That includes some of the most violent criminals in Russia, including Vyascheslav (no first name given), a former prosecutor who was sentenced to death. His crime was stabbing two women to death to see what it felt like. He was sentenced to death and came within a day of facing the firing squad.

There are only 170 prisoners at Petak Island, but they include the worst gangsters and murderers in Russia. That includes enforcers for the Russian mafia and professional killers.

Yet the guards that keep order in the facility carry nothing but a notebook and a can of mace. They don't need anything else because the prison is that tough.

Russia's Toughest Prison

Prisoners that go to Petak Island get two visits a year for the first 10 years of their sentence. If they stay for more than 10 years, prisoners get two more visits a year. Most prisoners don't get any visitors because the prison is so remote. Average Russians simply cannot afford to travel to visit the facility.

The isolation is a deliberate attempt to isolate Russia's worst prisoners from the underworld. Its location allows the Russian government to completely isolate the men imprisoned there.

Most of those men will spend their entire lives at Petak Island. The average prisoner there is serving a life sentence, and Russian President Vladimir Putin has pledged to keep the men in prison for at least 25 years.

Petak Island is so tough that many of the men there might like to see the death penalty restored. It is the only way that they will ever get out of Russia's toughest prison.

Bibliography

Foreign Prisoners (2007). Russian Gulags. Retrieved July 27, 2013, from Foreign Prisoners: http://www.foreignprisoners.com/prison-russia.html

Straus, J. (2004, August 10). Waiting for Death in Russia's Alcatraz. Retrieved July 27, 2013, from The Telegraph: http://www.telegraph.co.uk/news/worldnews/europe/russia/1469110/Waiting-for-death-in-Russias-Alcatraz.html

Riker's Island

New York City is so large that it has an entire island devoted to jails. Riker's Island, in the East River between Queens and the Bronx, actually houses 10 jails that are considered some of the toughest prisons in the United States. The island has been used as a jail since 1884 when the descendants of the original Dutch settlers of the island sold it to the city.

The only way on and off Riker's Island is the Francis Buono Bridge, which connects the island with Queens. Before the bridge was built in 1966, prisoners had to reach the island by ferry. Riker's Island is America's largest jail, and at any given time there can be as many as 13,000 inmates on the island.

One Island, Ten Jails

There are actually 10 jails on Riker's Island, each of which can house several hundred prisoners. That makes Riker's Island one of the largest penal facilities in the United States. No other American city has a detention facility as large or as complex as Riker's. The jails on Riker's Island include:

The James A. Thomas Center, formerly the House of Detention for Men. This is a maximum security jail that houses the toughest prisoners in New York City's system.

The North Infirmary Command, a hospital that houses sick prisoners, including many people with AIDS.

The Eric M. Taylor Center, which houses minimum security inmates.

The George Motchan Detention (or Correctional) Center, a former women's jail that is now used to house male prisoners.

The Robert N. Dovoren Center, which houses juvenile offenders.

The Anna M. Kross Center, which houses mentally ill prisoners and persons on drugs.

The Otis Bantum Correctional Center, another minimum security facility. Some of the prisoners at Otis Bantum actually sleep in two former Staten Island ferries, which were moored there to provide more beds.

The Rose M. Singer Center, a 1,700-bed jail for women. Among other things, this center contains a nursery that can house up to 25 infants.

The George R. Vierno Center, a medium-security jail.

The West Facility, the most modern jail in New York. It contains 140 special units designed to house prisoners with contagious diseases such as tuberculosis. This facility is currently sitting empty because of the recent drop in New York's crime rate.

Most of the facilities on Riker's Island are built on land that was used as garbage dumps during the 20th century and reclaimed from the East River. Even though it is part of New York City, the U.S. Postal Service considers Riker's Island a separate community called East Elmhurst, N.Y., which has its own zip code. That gives you an idea of how big the island is. Riker's Island is not the only U.S. prison that has its own zip code. The Louisiana State Penitentiary at Angola also has its own postal code.

Brutality on Riker's Island

As America's toughest jail in America's toughest city, Riker's Island has had its share of brutality. A case from 2012 is one of the most disturbing. *The New York Times* reported that the island's assistant chief of security ordered guards to beat and kick in the teeth of an inmate in July 2012.

The inmate, Jamal Lightfoot, was tackled, knocked to the ground, and beaten by at least nine officers. Lightfoot's injuries were so bad that prosecutors brought charges against the guards in state court in the Bronx. The prosecutors alleged that Perez ordered the beating because he thought Lightfoot looked tough.

Another version of the story states that Lightfoot was taken to a special pen after he tried to slash a corrections officer with a homemade knife. No decision has been reached in the case, which is still being tried. The Lightfoot incident is typical of brutality complaints that have been made against Riker's Island officials.

On May 14, 2012, two former Riker's Island officers, Capt. Sherman Graham and Deputy Warden Gail Lewis, were convicted of assaulting an inmate in front of 15 corrections officers in training. The two reportedly beat the inmate when he refused to undergo a strip search. The two were sentenced to 500 hours of community service and ordered to pay $1,000 fines.

The Enforcers and Other Strange Goings-On at Riker's

The New York City Department of Corrections itself admitted that as many as 150,000 Riker's Island inmates were subject to illegal strip searches. The searches carried out on nonviolent prisoners violated a court order the jail was under.

The Village Voice and *The New York Times* alleged that Riker's Island guards regularly used inmates as enforcers that terrorized prisoners that didn't follow the rules. The *Times* also claimed that the use of "enforcers", presumably gang members, led to at least seven lawsuits against the city. The enforcers were paid with cigarettes, marijuana, and alcohol. *The Village Voice* reported that enforcers were responsible for the death of at least one inmate, Steven Morales, who may have been killed by the enforcers.

The Inmate Who Sneaked Into Jail

The strangest story to come out of Riker's Island involves an ex-inmate named Matthew Matagrano. *The New York Times* reported that Matagrano, a registered sex offender, sneaked into Riker's Island and other New York jails in March 2013 by pretending to be a corrections officer. Matagrano made a fake identity card that indicated he was a city jail official. The card was so convincing that it fooled the guards at a number of facilities, possibly including Riker's Island.

He reportedly hung out for several hours in the jail, where he smoked cigarettes and stole a two-way radio. Prisoners apparently spotted Matagrano, but allowed him to stay because he gave them free cigarettes. Matagrano was later arrested and taken to Riker's Island. He might be the first prisoner in the facility's long and storied history who tried to sneak into New York's toughest jail.

Bibliography

Corrections History (n.d.). Ten Jails on Riker's Island. Retrieved July 24, 2013, from Corrections History:
http://www.correctionhistory.org/html/chronicl/nycdoc/html/jailist1.html

Goldstein, J., & Leonard, R. (2013, June 26). Riker's Island Security Chief is Charged with Ordering Brutal Assault on Inmate. Retrieved July 24, 2013, from The New York Times:
http://www.nytimes.com/2013/06/27/nyregion/correction-officers-and-supervisors-charged-in-beating-at-rikers.html?ref=rikersislandprisoncomplex&_r=0

Schwirtz, M. (2013, March 3). Ex-Inmate Sneaked Into Jail by Impersonating Official, Authorities Say. Retrieved July 24, 2013, from The New York Times:
http://cityroom.blogs.nytimes.com/2013/03/02/ex-inmate-sneaked-into-jail-by-impersonating-official-authorities-say/?ref=rikersislandprisoncomplex

Wikipedia (n.d.). Riker's Island. Retrieved July 24, 2013, from Wikipedia:
http://en.wikipedia.org/wiki/Rikers_Island

Tadmor Prison

The regime of the Assad family, the late Syrian President Hafesz al-Assad and his son and successor Bashar, has long been considered one of the world's most brutal dictatorships. It is no surprise that Assad and his son are also proprietors of one of the world's most brutal penitentiaries, the Tadmor Prison, located just outside the city of Hamas.

Tadmor was built by French colonialists in the 1930s as an instrument of oppression against the Syrian people. Hafesz al-Assad not only kept Tadmor open but also expanded it to lock his enemies in it. When Assad expanded Tadmor, he employed a method used by Joseph Stalin—he housed political prisoners and common criminals together. One of the main reasons for this was to maintain the fiction that political opponents are actually criminals and deserving of punishment.

Criminals were given a new prison to live in, while members of the opposition party, the Muslim Brotherhood, were housed in the old section of the prison. The prison was also terribly overcrowded. Dissident Bara Sarraj, who was imprisoned there in the 1980s, said 2,400 prisoners were sometimes locked in cellblocks built for 100 inmates.

The Symphony of Fear

In his autobiography, Sarraj gave Tadmor the very sinister and appropriate nickname "the Symphony of Fear." Authorities at Tadmor went out of their way to dehumanize and terrorize their prisoners.

The guards denied prisoners any contact with the outside world, such as radios and any sort of diversion like books. The goons figured out how to use boredom as a weapon. To add to the monotony, no salt or spices for the food were allowed. Small humiliations were used to strip prisoners of all dignity, such as denying prisoners needles and thread needed to repair clothing.

Sarraj also describes a travesty of democracy. Inside Tadmor, prisoners in the facility had one right denied to the Syrian people. They could elect a leader or president among themselves. It isn't clear whether this was a cruel game played by guards or simply something bored prisoners did to keep amused.

The Massacre

The worst atrocity at Tadmor took place on June 27, 1980. A day earlier, an assassin had gotten close enough to President Assad to toss a grenade at him. The assassin failed and Assad lived.

The next day, at 6:30 a.m., 60 Syrian soldiers, commanded by Assad's brother, Rifaat Assad, arrived at Tadmor. The soldiers were part of the "Defense Companies," the Assad family's personal goon squad.

Rifaat split the soldiers into units then ordered them to go into the section that housed political prisoners and kill every prisoner in sight. The killing was carried out in retaliation for the attempt on Assad's life, which was blamed on the Muslim Brotherhood.

Human rights groups estimated that between 500 and 800 unarmed men were shot down, but Syrian dissidents thought the death toll might have been much higher. Sarraj thought as many as 2,400 people might have been shot.

Horrific Tortures and Crimes

The brutality at Tadmor had been described as unbelievable. Sarraj said he saw prisoners dragged to death with a rope and chopped up with an axe.

Members of the Muslim Brotherhood were beaten daily. Other prisoners were whipped for as long as a week. Some prisoners were also kept blindfolded all the time as a means of humiliating them.

Hangings were a regular part of life at Tadmor. Those hanged were first tried in a kangaroo court in which the prison's warden, an Assad stooge, served as the judge. Like much else at Tadmor, the court was a travesty of civilized life.

Tadmor Closes for 10 Years and Reopens

Tadmor prison reportedly closed down in 2001. It closed because Hafez al Assad died and was succeeded by his supposedly liberal son, Bashar, who closed the prison as part of his reforms, but the reforms were a cruel travesty. Bashar al-Assad wanted to show the world that he was a liberal reformer, which he was not. Like his father, Bashar was dedicated to maintaining the family's power and wealth at all costs.

In 2011 the Arab Spring uprisings, which brought down such despots as Muammar Gaddafi and Egypt's Hosni Mubarak, swept the Middle East. The uprising produced the opposite results in Syria. The regime became more oppressive and brutal. Bashar al-Assad reopened Tadmor and began putting his political enemies into it again.

Syria is currently in the middle of a bloody civil war between the people and the Assad family and its military apparatus. The status of Tadmor is not clear because Hamas is in the center of the fighting. It isn't known which side controls it or if rebels or Assad forces are using it as a detention center. It is possible that Assad supporters might be locked up in their regime's most infamous prison.

The future of Tadmor is uncertain because the outcome of Syria's civil war has not been decided. The rebels haven't been able to overcome Assad's heavy weapons, but Assad's forces lack the manpower to control the country. Recently, both the United States and Russia have started arming both sides.

That means Tadmor may be open for the foreseeable future, even if Bashar al-Assad is killed or driven from power. Its fate, like that of Syria, will probably be decided on the battlefield.

Bibliography

Hilleary, C. (2012, June 27). Syria's Tadmor Prison Massacre: Reliving Horrors of 32 Years Past. Retrieved July 25, 2013, from Middle East Voices: http://middleeastvoices.voanews.com/2012/06/syrias-tadmor-prison-massacre-reliving-horrors-of-32-years-past-81070/

Human Rights Watch (1996, April). Syria's Tadmor Prison. Retrieved July 25, 2013, from Human Rights Watch: http://www.hrw.org/reports/1996/Syria2.htm